T0380824

Oxford Mice

By Trudy McNair

Archway Publishing books may be ordered through booksellers or by contacting:

Archway Publishing
1663 Liberty Drive
Bloomington, IN 47403
www.archwaypublishing.com
844-669-3957

Because of the dynamic nature of the Internet, any web addresses or links contained in this book may have changed since publication and may no longer be valid. The views expressed in this work are solely those of the author and do not necessarily reflect the views of the publisher, and the publisher hereby disclaims any responsibility for them.

ISBN: 978-1-6657-3820-0 (sc)
ISBN: 978-1-6657-3821-7 (hc)
ISBN: 978-1-6657-3822-4 (e)

Print information available on the last page.

Archway Publishing rev. date: 03/07/2023

Introduction and Historical Overview

Hello. My name is William McMouse, but everybody calls me Will. I come from a long line of Oxford mice, who live in Oxford, England.

As long as anyone can remember there have been mice from the McMouse clan living in Oxford.

Rumor has it that my ancestors originally came from Scotland, that the family left through a hole in Hadrian's Wall that was built by the Romans to keep the Scots out and the British people in.

I am not sure if I was named after William I, better known as William the Conqueror, the first Norman (French) king of England, who invaded England in 1066, a date that every English school girl and boy (and mouse) has memorized (more about that later).

My ancestors escaping from Scotland through Hadrian's Wall.

Or, I might have been named after the bard William Shakespeare, who lived in the sixteenth century. One of my ancestors ran across the stage during a Shakespearean production at Oxford and caused quite a commotion. Some of my ancestors were monks, artists, soldiers, scribes (medieval copiers of manuscripts), chroniclers (historians), and even kings and queens.

It is believed that my family descends from an ancient line of Scottish kings and queens, who had a unique gene and were born without whiskers. I learned about my family's and Oxford's history as a wee tyke from my father reading to me from a big green book.

It's nice to grow up in such a historical place, but it can be a little daunting at times.

When I think of the hardships my ancestors went through, I feel a little spoilt.

I have a nice view of an Oxford street from my bedroom window, and I love listening to the church bells from the many churches in Oxford, but enough about me.

I would like to share with you the history of Oxford as told to me by my family and that was written about in my ancestors' diaries, which my father has carefully preserved in our library.
I live with my family at Exeter College, which is part of Oxford University (see Part III).

Exeter has a prime location between Broad Street and High Street.

Picture of my great-grandparents' wedding.

I think I inherited my adventurous spirit from my ancestors, beginning with the ones who crossed Hadrian's Wall.

As a young lad, I had a recurring dream that I was floating in the air on a leaf and being watched by birds. I think it meant that I was supposed to live my life without fear because I would have friends to help me and the protection of Mother Nature.

By the way, my great-grandparents were born in the 1950s and grew up after World War II. Oxford wasn't bombed during World War II so the mice at Oxford were fortunate.

Oxford and Oxford's mice went through many difficult and dangerous times in their history, but let's start from the beginning.

Oxford began with the establishment of a river crossing or fording (an old word for crossing over) for oxen on the River Thames about 900 A.D., hence the name Oxford. The rivers Cherwell and Thames flow through Oxford.

Interesting tidbit: The section of the River Thames that flows through Oxford is often called the Isis from the Latinized name Thamesis.

Oxford was an important port on the River Thames and a crossroads trading town with many coaching inns that were inhabited by Oxford's regular folk, including many mice, who raided the dining rooms in search of food.

Today, the river is filled with barges. Some people live on the barges. Oxford students also use the river to punt (using long poles to navigate the river in narrow boats).

Oxford was also a very religious town. A number of monasteries and religious houses were established in and around Oxford.

Oxford grew up around a Saxon monastery dedicated to St. Frideswide (a name meaning "Peace-Strong"), Oxford's patron saint and the patron saint of Oxford University (see Part III). Her feast day is October 19, the date of her death in 727 A.D.

St. Frideswide was the only child and the daughter of a Saxon king who ruled an area around Oxford. So she was originally a princess before she became a saint.

She was motherless and looked after by nuns, who taught her to read and write and play the lyre and harp.

Her father wanted her to marry a Mercian king (Mercia was a kingdom in the English Midlands from the sixth to the tenth centuries), but she was bound to celibacy and wanted to be a nun.

When she heard from her ladies that her father was arranging her marriage, she wept and decided to flee. No one saw her leave, not even a mouse.

She slipped out of her father's castle with her ladies in the dark of night and fled to Oxford where she found a boat. She rowed up the River Thames with her ladies until they came to a tiny hamlet.

She was taken in by devout women and helped them care for the poor and sick. She performed miracles healing the sick and blind.

Hearing her father was ill over her flight, she returned to her father, who allowed her to become a nun. She became the first abbess of what is called a "double-monastery," a place for nuns and monks. Some of my ancestors were monks and nuns at the St. Frideswide Priory.

The tradition of writing down the history of Oxford began in the Renaissance (1400-1600) by my ancestors.

Part II: The Norman Conquest

One of the most important events in English history is the conquest of England by William the Conqueror in 1066 A.D.

William the Conqueror came from Normandy, France, and conquered the Anglo-Saxon people living in England at the time.

Interesting tidbit: The Normans' ancestors were actually Vikings (a Viking is a pirate and plunderer from Sweden, Norway, or Denmark); they spoke Norse, hence the name Normans or Norsemen.

The Normans were given the area in northern France called Normandy by the French king in 911 A.D. so they would stop invading the rest of France.

Castles were used to help complete the conquest of England. By building castles in certain areas and towns like Oxford, the Normans could control the population as well as trade and territory.

The Normans developed castle-building in the tenth and eleventh centuries.

Interesting tidbit: To be defined as a castle, the castle must be fortified for defense and also serve as the living quarters of the lord and lady and their family.

The motte-and-bailey style of castle developed in Europe from the tenth century onwards and was introduced to England by the Normans.

The famous "Tower of London" castle begun by William the Conqueror.

These early castles were build of wood and consisted of a motte (an earthen mound flattened on the top) where the keep (the fortified tower where the lord and lady and their family lived) was located.

The motte was attached to one or two baileys.

The bailey was an enclosed courtyard on a smaller mound where the animals and soldiers lived.

The bailey contained a number of buildings such as a chapel, kitchen, barracks (where the soldiers slept), and stables for the animals.

The whole castle was surrounded by a wooden fence of logs called a palisade. Castles were also usually surrounded by a dry ditch or moat with water.

Stone-built keeps and walls soon replaced the wooden ones.

Hundreds of motte-and-bailey castles were built by the Normans in England as well as in Scotland and Ireland.

My uncle explained to me that Anglo-Norman warfare mainly consisted of raiding and besieging castles to take control of the enemy's territory. Slow sieges were usually preferred to direct assaults on a castle. Pitched battles in the open were usually avoided.

A Norman knight and baron named Robert d'Oilly, who arrived with William the Conqueror in 1066, claimed Oxford as his personal prize in the conquest. Oilly built Oxford Castle and turned Oxford into a Norman stronghold.

Oxford Castle was built on the western side of Oxford. The castle had a moat and was meant to dominate the town. The original wooden motte-and-bailey castle was replaced by a stone one in the eleventh century.

The keep and bailey buildings are gone, but the motte survives and a well chamber. The tallest of the castle's towers, St. George's Tower, built in stone in 1074, still stands today.

The tower is next to a part of the Thames which served as the western part of the moat.

St. George's Tower includes a crypt chapel with solid pillars and arches that was dedicated to St. George.

Some of the fanciest castles were built in France during the Renaissance Period.

The Normans brought knighthood to England.

The date 1066 marks the beginning of the Age of Knights. Mounted, armored knights were supported by infantry (foot soldiers).

Interesting tidbit: The knights originated in France and always rode on horseback. The Code of Chivalry, a code of honor for the knights, comes from *cheval*, the French word for horse. Their early armor consisted of chainmail, which is hundreds of metal rings sewn together. Later the chainmail was replaced by plate armor.

William the Conqueror took much of the Anglo-Saxons' land and gave it to the Normans, making the Anglo-Saxons pretty upset.

Anglo-Saxon mice felt they were also badly treated by the Norman invaders and refused to speak French.

Two knights in plate armor

A group of Norman French-speaking mice came over with William. It is rumored that these mice, who spoke French like the Normans, tried to impose their language on my Anglo-Saxon ancestors in Oxford, but they were unsuccessful.

Although French became the language of the court and upper classes, my family still spoke good old-fashioned Anglo-Saxon English with a few French words thrown in for good measure.

Interesting tidbit: There are many Norman-French words that made their way into the English language. Many are words associated with the court and the military such as soldier, army, and administration.

24

The Normans were religious and set up a monastic community at Oxford Castle.

Some of my ancestors took up holy orders and lived in the monks quarters in the castle.

The monastery had a reputation for learning, and it was at the castle monastery of Oxford that Geoffrey of Monmouth wrote the famous *History of the Kings of England* telling the story of the legendary King Arthur.

Family lore has one line of my family living at King Arthur's court at Camelot in southern England in the fifth century, the time of Arthur. My favorite bedtime stories were about King Arthur and his Knights of the Round Table and the search for the holy grail.

Rumor has it that two of my ancestors were the first to discover the "sword in the stone" which the teenaged Arthur pulled out and was proclaimed king.

Part III: The "Anarchy," The First English Civil War

The English have fought three major civil wars: the Normans fought a civil war between the supporters of Stephen and the supporters of Matilda, which will be the focus of this chapter.

The second civil war, the War of the Roses, was fought in the fifteenth century, between the Lancastrians (symbolized by the red rose) and the Yorkists (symbolized by the white rose).

Thankfully, Oxford did not play a major part in that very bloody conflict.

The third civil war, the first modern civil war, was fought in the 1640s and will be discussed in Part IV.

Oxford played a key role in the first and third civil wars.

Oxford mice remember the time of the first civil war, often called the "Anarchy," which lasted from 1135 to 1153, with great sadness.

The Anarchy caused great devastation and suffering. The records of the Anarchy were kept by chroniclers, who were pretty much in favor of one side or another, but I will try to give an unbiased account.

The conflict started because William the Conqueror's grandson, the son and heir of Henry I, William the Conqueror's son, died when the famous "White Ship" sailing from Normandy to England sank in 1120.

Henry I tried to install his daughter, the Empress Matilda (she is called the empress because her first husband, who died, was the Holy Roman Emperor), but, when Henry died, his nephew Stephen took the throne, even though Stephen had sworn an oath to support Matilda. So much for oaths.

King Stephen instructing two of his knights clad in chainmail.

Interesting tidbit: English monarchs are numbered consecutively by name. For example, there have been eight English kings with the name of Henry: the first one was the son of William the Conqueror; the last one, the most famous, was Henry VIII, who lived in the sixteenth century and is famous for having six wives.

Matilda arrived in England from Normandy with 140 knights in 1139. Matilda's second husband, Geoffrey of Anjou, did not go to England during the war, but he conquered Normandy and became recognized as the Duke of Normandy in 1144.

Matilda was supported by her half-brother, Robert of Gloucester, and by most of Oxford's mice, including my ancestors.

In the southwest of England, Matilda's supporters built a string of castles, and Stephen built a new chain of castles around Cambridge (later the site of a famous university).

Matilda was staying at Arundel Castle when it was besieged by Stephen.

Stephen, for some reason, agreed to release Matilda during the siege of Arundel. It is unclear why. Maybe because of chivalry or because he was more worried about her half-brother Robert.

The Catholic pope in Rome confirmed Stephen as king. This was a time when pretty much everyone in Europe was Catholic. Stephen also had the support of the Catholic church in England.

Stephen was a well-liked, popular king. He once gave up a castle to secure the release of one of his best men.

Stephen relied heavily on his wife, who was also named Matilda, especially when Stephen was captured at the Battle of Lincoln in 1141 by the army of Robert of Gloucester. He was held at Bristol Castle.

His wife Matilda maintained his cause and his army while he was imprisoned. She was able to capture Robert of Gloucester so they agreed to exchange Robert for Stephen and both were set free. Makes sense to me.

When Stephen was imprisoned, Matilda thought she would become queen, but an uprising of Stephen's supporters in London forced her to flee to Oxford. Stephen had built a screen of castles on the way to London.

The baron of Oxford Castle supported Matilda, and, in 1141, Matilda marched to Oxford to base her campaign at the castle.

Stephen marched to Oxford and besieged the town and Matilda in the castle. Oxford was protected by walls and part of the River Thames, but Stephen attacked across the river, swimming part of the way.

Queen Matilda's escape from Oxford Castle. Note the worried look on Matilda's face.

Stephen set up two make-shift castles with siege mounds beside Oxford Castle on which he placed siege engines and waited for supplies at Oxford Castle to run low.

Empress Matilda was surrounded by Stephen's forces, and things looked bleak for her.

Oxford mice remember a cold and dark December night just before Christmas when Matilda fled Oxford Castle in the middle of the night during the siege of Oxford.

The mice fearfully watched from a window in the castle as Matilda crossed the frozen castle Mill Stream, a stream off the River Thames, on foot.

According to my ancestors, she was wearing her night clothes, which were white to blend in with the snow, and was accompanied by several knights. The castle surrendered to Stephen the next day after her daring escape.

By the late 1140s, the civil war was over. In 1147, Robert died, and, in 1148, Matilda gave up and returned to Normandy.

Interesting tidbit: Although the wives of the kings are England are called queens, England has had six queens in their own right, but Matilda is not counted among them because she was never officially the queen. England has had two Marys, one Anne, one Victoria, and two Elizabeths who were queens.

Matilda promoted her son, Henry, to be the future king of England.

Henry invaded England in 1153; Stephen lost the town of Oxford and made peace with Stephen, who recognized Henry as his heir. They sealed their treaty with a kiss of peace in Winchester Cathedral in 1153. Stephen died in 1154, and Henry was crowned King Henry II.

Henry was a dynamic person. At age 18, he married the equally dynamic and powerful Queen Eleanor of Aquitaine, the divorced wife of the king of France.

The crowning of Henry II by the archbishop.

Eleanor was the wife of two kings and the mother of two kings: Richard the Lionheart (Richard I) and John I, both of whom were born at Oxford in the twelfth century.

Henry II had many scandals. He famously imprisoned Eleanor after she was involved in a plot against him with her former husband, the king of France. When Henry died, Eleanor was let out of prison by the new king, Richard the Lionheart.

Another famous event was the quarrel between King Henry II and Thomas a' Becket, who used to be Henry's friend, but then he sided with the church against Henry after Henry made Becket archbishop of Canterbury, the highest church office in England.

The Oxford mice were divided between their support of Henry and Becket. The more Catholic and religious mice supported Becket, who was eventually killed by four of Henry's knights in Canterbury Cathedral. Henry was blamed for Becket's death.

Interesting tidbit: The great playwright William Shakespeare never wrote plays about the Anarchy or about Henry and Eleanor or Henry and Becket, but he wrote a number of plays about the period before and during The War of the Roses, a civil war for control of the throne between the Lancastrians and the Yorkists that lasted from 1455 to 1485.

King Richard II created the title the Duke of York, first bestowed on his uncle in 1385. Richard II lost the throne in 1399 to his cousin, who became King Henry IV, a Lancastrian. His deposition by Henry IV was the underlying cause of the War of the Roses in the fifteenth century.

Shakespeare wrote ten history plays, many about English kings, such as the doomed Yorkist kings Richard II and Richard III, who were overthrown and killed, and the Lancastrian father and son Henry IV and Henry V.

Richard III was the last king of the House of York. He lost his throne to the Lancastrian Henry VII, who united the Yorkists and Lancastrians in marriage and began the Tudor dynasty.

Part IV: Oxford University

Oxford is most famous became it is the site of Oxford University, the oldest university in the English-speaking world and many would say the most prestigious university in the world.

The first European universities developed in the twelfth century. The earliest four universities were two in Italy, the University of Paris, and Oxford.

The nineteenth-century poet Matthew Arnold, called Oxford "that sweet city with her dreaming spires." There are lots of spires at Oxford and one famous dome, that of the Radcliffe Camera (more about that later).

The university grew rapidly after 1167 when Henry II ordered the English students who were studying at the University of Paris to come home during the Becket controversy.

The students came to Oxford to study and the town grew. By 1216, there were over 1,000 masters (teachers) and students.

By end of the thirteenth century, there were about 3,000 people living in Oxford (divided equally between the people associated with the university and the people associated with the town) and about 30,000 mice.

Many religious orders, such as the Franciscans, settled in Oxford during the thirteenth century and maintained halls (boarding houses for students). Gradually, most of the halls were replaced by colleges.

Oxford is made up of separate institutions called colleges that are made up of students and teachers, but all of the students take their degrees from Oxford University. Pretty confusing.

My home Exeter College is famous for its chapel, which displays a famous tapestry of the Three Wise Men giving gifts to the Baby Jesus. It was created by the nineteenth-century artist Edward Byrne-Jones.

Some of the buildings of the St. Frideswide Priory were incorporated into Christ Church following the dissolution of the monasteries in 1539.

In 1542, Henry VIII made the ancient priory church of St. Frideswide into the smallest cathedral in England.

Christ Church has both a chapel and a cathedral in one, and both the cathedral and college became known as Christ Church College.

Christ Church is the site of a cathedral (the home of a bishop) and the center of the diocese (an area ruled by a bishop) of Oxford.

Christ Church cathedral has a stained glass window designed by the English artist Edward Burne-Jones (who attended Exeter College) in the 1850s.

Interesting tidbit: The Christ Church Picture Gallery has over 200 pictures of old masters and was the inspiration for the dining hall of Hogwarts School in the Harry Potter movies.

The earliest colleges began in the thirteenth century. Colleges were founded by bishops, kings, and wealthy patrons, who established colleges as self-contained scholarly communities.

Some students supported themselves by begging, and some were supported by their home churches or monasteries or by a wealthy patron. Many students had their room and board provided by the colleges, which are scattered over the city of Oxford.

The first three colleges at Oxford were founded in the thirteenth century, and the others grew up piecemeal.

In 1264, the first college, Merton College, was founded by a benefactor, Walter de Merton, to create a new kind of permanent institution.

The colleges are self-governing and are endowed with land and other assets.

The colleges are designed around a quadrangle (quad for short), and Merton has the oldest quad called the "Mob Quad" that was built between 1288-1378. The reason why it is called the Mob Quad are obscure, but it may be a humorous description of the occupants. Merton also has the oldest college buildings.

The colleges have a monastic feeling to them, and the quads are similar to the cloisters in monasteries, which are spaces surrounded by a covered walkway or open arcade along the walls of buildings forming a quadrangle. Whew! That was a long sentence!

While a quad at Oxford is usually framed by buildings such as a chapel, dining hall, library, and dormitory for students minus the walkway or arcade, there are also traditional cloisters called quads at Oxford.

As I mentioned earlier, I live with my family at Exeter College, which was founded in 1314 by a bishop to educate clergymen for the church.

I love hanging out at the Exeter quad. One time I saw a group of ducks on the quad with the mother duck acting like a crossing guard so her little ones could pass. It was so cute.

"All Souls" College was founded by the Archbishop of Canterbury in 1437 as a war memorial to mourn those killed in the Hundred Years War (1337-1453) between France and England. England won. Yea.

A mother duck stopping traffic at the Exeter quad.

Each college generally has its own library, dining hall, chapel, and dormitory, but all share the main library and some other buildings like the Sheldonian Theater that was built between 1664 and 1669 and is used for special events and lectures.

The theater was designed by the greatest of all English architects, Sir Christopher Wren, who was a student at All Souls. Wren was one of the founders of the Royal Society in London in 1660 and a professor of astronomy. Two of his most famous architectural achievements are St. Paul's Cathedral in London and Tom Tower at Christ Church College, the grandest of the colleges, which was founded in 1546.

Tom Tower houses great Tom a six-ton bell, and its quad is named Tom Quad. It is the largest quad at Oxford.

As I mentioned before, it is believed Christ Church is located on the site of the original St. Frideswide Priory and Saxon church. St. Frideswide's shrine was vandalized during the dissolution of the Catholic monasteries in 1539 by Henry VIII after he made himself head of the new church of England, the Anglican Church.

To obtain a Bachelors, Master's, or Doctorate degree, students had to endure years of study. Books were very expensive and were hand written until the invention of printing with moveable type in Germany in 1455.

Most undergraduate learning at Oxford is based on the tutorial system so students meet with their tutors rather than attend classes although they also attend lectures.

Student life was harsh, and there were frequent epidemics. Students complained about the bad food, high rents, arrogant professors, and lack of jobs after graduation. Sounds familiar.

Learning began with a study of the past and reading the texts of authors such as Greek philosophers like Aristotle.

Public debates between individual professors and their students were common. During the Middle Ages, the university people spoke and wrote in Latin. Pretty confusing stuff.

Graduate students were subjected to a grueling oral examination that was much like a jousting tournament at the end of their study. Once a student had received a Master's degree, he (there were no female students allowed until the end of the nineteenth century) could teach at any university or have a career in the church.

The deer park at Magdalen College. (They look pretty content).

I love to have a ramble or stroll on Christ Church meadow. Three of the most beautiful places in Oxford are the Christ Church meadow, the deer part at Magdalen College, and the Christ Church garden that was laid out in 1926 to commemorate the members of Christ Church College who died in World War I.

Lewis Carroll (his real name was Charles Dodgson), who wrote *Alice in Wonderland*, was a mathematics tutor at Christ Church. His stories were inspired by the daughter of the dean of Christ Church; her name was Alice. My ancestors would sit on the banks of the river listening to Mr. Carroll tell his stories to Alice and her friends.

Christ Church has produced sixteen prime ministers of Britain, including Winston Churchill, who was prime minister during World War II.

I have a cousin named Winston, who was named after Winston Churchill, but I don't have much to do with that side of the family because they think they are the "cat's meow" so to speak.

If a master gave a cheap banquet after obtaining a degree, he might have his classes boycotted by students, who were always hungry.

Sometimes it was dangerous to be a mouse living in Oxford, especially during the civil wars and the so-called "Town-and-Gown riots." There was lots of conflict between the Town-and-Gown people living in Oxford although the Town-and-Gown mice got along quite well.

The riots usually began when the townspeople or the gowns people got fed up with each other when they were served some bad beer or wine at a tavern or inn and started to riot.

Interesting tidbit: Wine and beer (called mead, an ancient alcoholic drink that was similar to beer) were the two main drinks at Oxford, and many colleges are proud of their wine cellars. There is a long history of brewing at Oxford. By 1874, there were nine breweries in Oxford. Several colleges had private breweries until 1889.

A typical Oxford tavern that usually had a few rooms for rent. They were popular with Oxford's mice as a good source for food.

Oxford grew in power because of the Town-and-Gown riots. In the beginning, the university did not own much land or property so the students and university people lived off of the local economy and rented halls and other buildings. The first Town-and-Gown riot occurred at the University of Paris in 1200.

In 1209, after a fierce riot at Oxford, a group of unhappy scholars left Oxford and headed north about 100 miles up the road and founded Cambridge University, which also had its share of Town-and-Gown riots.

Most of Oxford's mice stayed put because 100 miles is a long way to walk for a mouse unless they could hitch a ride somehow. The riots were followed by an increase in the rights of the university at the expense of the townspeople.

In large part because of the riots, members of the university clustered behind high, fortress-like walls that surrounded their colleges.

The worst riot in Oxford began in 1355 on Scholastica's Day at a tavern when fighting erupted over some bad beer. It lasted a month, and things got pretty bad.

About twenty inns were pillaged, many college halls were burned, and at least 60 students were killed. The king forced the mayor and other townspeople to pay for all the damages and perform a humiliating annual penance for 480 years on Scholastica's Day and swear to observe the privileges of the university.

When bad things happened at Oxford, my ancestors always looked back and said: "This would never have happened in the old king's day."

King Henry III turned part of Oxford Castle into a prison, specifically for holding troublesome university students.

Oxford's Christ Church meadow was a
popular place for "mouse courting."

In 1605, Oxford was still a walled city, but several colleges had been built outside of the city walls.

Today, there are over forty self-governing halls and colleges at Oxford: thirty-eight colleges and six halls.

The first of four women's colleges was established in 1878, and women were given full rights to take degrees in 1920.

There were many famous people who went to Oxford. The nineteenth-century Romantic poet Shelley was expelled from Oxford for being an atheist. There is now a tacky statue of Shelley at University College where he attended as a first-year student.

The writer C.S. Lewis was also a student at University College and a Fellow at Magdalen College; J.R.R. Tolkien, who wrote *The Lord of the Rings*, was a student at Exeter College from 1913 to 1917 and later professor of English at Merton College.

Interesting tidbits: Oxford has the oldest botanical garden in Great Britain founded in 1621.

Thomas Bodley, a fellow of Merton, in 1598, began work on the Bodleian Library in 1598; the library opened in 1602. The Bodleian Library houses about eleven million volumes over miles of shelving. Pretty impressive.

The smartest members of my family like to hang out at the Bodleian Library where so many famous scholars go to read books and look at manuscripts.

I've never been there because we have a nice library at home, thanks to my scholarly father.

The famous domed Radcliffe Camera is part of the Bodleian Library. The camera (which is a type of chamber) was named after a royal physician and was built between 1737 and 1748.

Oxford also has the largest university press in the world.

The Ashmolean Museum, founded in 1683, houses the jewel of King Alfred the Great. The Ashmolean is the world's first university museum and the oldest museum in the United Kingdom.

The late nineteenth and early twentieth century witnessed the rise of organized sports. Oxford has cricket (a game a bit like baseball) and rowing clubs.

The famous Radcliffe Camera

Sometimes I like to play football (soccer to you Americans) on the quad at night with my friends or cruise on my boat on a nearby pond. Punting on the Thames/Isis and Cherwell rivers is popular with students, and rowing races are popular as well.

One time I was seen roaming the halls by several housekeepers who take care of the students. They are called scouts (not a very nice name if you ask me), and they scooted me out of the building at the end of a broom.

My side of the family is more adventurous. A group of Oxford mice, myself included, like to put on our black robes. Students wore coarse, black gowns with a hood, which often served as a kind of "backpack" to carry their food, notes, and other materials. The professors (also called masters or dons) also wore black gowns.

My friends and I wander around at night in our black robes so we can't be seen. Oxford's many gargoyles (often scary statues on a building) can be quite frightening at night.

Even more scary, one time I got lost in the Pitt River Museum, which was founded in 1884 and houses archeological and anthropological artifacts (an artifact is something made by people); the bones were really creepy.

But enough about me, back to my ancestors.

Not all gargoyles are scary. I actually have my own personal gargoyle who is fun to hang out with. It was carved by a French-Norman mouse who I befriended even though we don't agree on Anglo-French politics. I taught him Anglo-Saxon English.

I call my gargoyle "Twinkle Toes" because I like the way his toes curve. He is always there for me when I need to talk to someone.

Interesting tidbit:

A gargoyle is technically a waterspout as opposed to a statue, which is called a grotesque, but I call my grotesque a gargoyle because I like the name better because there is nothing grotesque about my friend.

Part V: The Third Civil War between Parliament and King Charles I

Interesting tidbit: Oxford suffered during the Protestant Reformation and had statues and stained glass windows smashed by orders of Henry VIII.

Several of my ancestors were artists who painted portraits of the kings and queens of England. Elizabeth I was very fussy about her portraits and image.

Elizabeth's older half-sister Queen Mary, the queen before Elizabeth, is called "Bloody Mary" because she was Catholic and England was Protestant after King Henry VIII broke with the Catholic Church. So, Mary burned about 300 Protestants at the stake, hence her name Bloody Mary.

Oxford was the place where the most famous three men were burned by Mary. They were two Protestant bishops and the archbishop of Canterbury. They were tried for heresy and burnt at the stake in 1555 on Broad Street, and there is a martyrs' memorial there that was built in 1843.

Elizabeth I was the last Tudor monarch and then came the Stuarts. The second Stuart king, Charles I, got into trouble with Parliament (the English legislative branch of government), and the Third English Civil War broke out in 1642. It was a religious and political war that lasted from 1642 until 1649.

Charles was having trouble with the Scots and members of Parliament over religious matters, taxation, and other matters, which together sparked the war.

From 1642 to 1646, Oxford was the royal capital and military headquarters of Charles and his forces after Charles was expelled from London by Parliament in 1642. The colleges were taken over by the king, who was housed at Christ Church College.

Oxford's gown mice and the university people sided with the king, but most of the townspeople and town mice sided with Parliament.

The soldiers who supported the king were called Cavaliers; they were mounted soldiers with longer hair than the supporters of Parliament, who were called Roundheads because of their round, short haircuts.

As many soldiers died in warfare as by disease. Families, including my own, were torn apart, some supporting the king and some Parliament.

Some letters from the common soldiers have survived since more people could read and write. One soldier described the thousands of musket balls flying through the air as like "hailstones."

Women played a large role in the war defending their homes and castles and even serving as soldiers disguised as men.

Charles' wife, the French queen, returned to France in 1644. She was very courageous in support of her husband.

Some Royalist mice dressed up like the king's men and served as a network of spies for the king, leaving messages for the king's men.

Since the time of the First Civil War, canons and guns in the form of muskets were invented. The war was fought mainly with swords, muskets, and with twenty-foot pikes.

Military strategy had changed as well. The Third Civil War witnessed frequent battles, some of them involving as many as 15,000 to 20,000 soldiers on each side. The blocks of infantry faced each other surrounded by the cavalry.

But sieges were still common. There were 198 sieges in the war, and more people died in sieges than in battles. There were many besieged fortresses, strongholds, and castles. Many beautiful castles were destroyed.

The average siege of a town or castle lasted 54 days, but they could last as much as five months.

In 1646, the Parliamentarians besieged Oxford, and the city was occupied. They refortified Oxford Castle and destroyed much of the medieval castle.

The Siege of Oxford (May 1644-June 1646) during the English Civil War consisted of three short conflicts or sieges, which ended with Royalist-controlled Oxford being taken by the Parliamentarians in June 1646.

During the first siege, on June 3, 1644, the king escaped; like the Empress Matilda before him in the First English Civil War, the king escaped disguised under the cover of darkness.

In 1645, the king was captured by a Scottish force and eventually handed over to Parliament. In January 1649, Charles was sentenced to death after a trial by Parliament in London; he was found guilty of treason and beheaded on January 30, 1649, a very sad day.

The mice watched in horror as Oxford was surrendered, and the mice learned that the king was later taken prisoner. One brave mouse stood behind a red curtain to show his loyalty as the king was told he was no longer safe at Oxford. The king was taken to London where he was beheaded.

Note the sad look on the king's face when told he must leave his headquarters at Oxford.

My ancestors remember receiving word of the king's execution and bursting into tears. Many never got over the shock and loss.

I think even the Roundhead mice were pretty sad that the king lost his head. Mice in general do not believe in violence, but they are brave creatures who will defend their home and country.

It was a very costly war in terms of lives, money, and property lost. Much of England lay in ruins, and towns and villages were devastated. A popular song said it was "a world upside down."

The future King Charles II, the son of Charles I, had escaped capture in 1651 at age sixteen by hiding in an oak tree, which is why there are so many Royal Oak pubs in England.

He fled to France and returned to England in 1660 to retake the crown during the "Glorious Revolution."

Oxford mice monks mourning the loss of King Charles I and entering their chapel to pray for his soul.

Oxford housed the court of Charles II during the plague years of 1665-1666.

After the horrible civil war of the seventeenth century, the eighteenth and nineteenth centuries were more peaceful for Oxford until the outbreak of World War I in the early twentieth century.

During World War I (1914-1918), students, faculty, and staff enlisted, and many university buildings became hospitals and military training camps.

One last tidbit of interesting information: William Morris, the most important car manufacturer in Britain for many years, based his factory at his hometown of Oxford. He started work at a bicycle shop at age fifteen and built his first car in 1912.

His produced his first car at the Oxford factory in 1913. The popular Morris mini was launched in 1959 and was produced until 2000.

Years ago, some student discarded his old Morris toy cars in a box that was discovered by my uncle so I grew up racing Morris cars on the roof of my building.

The badge of a Morris car shows an ox fording the River Isis (an image which is also on the coat of arms of Oxford) so this is a good place to end our trip through time.

I hope you enjoyed learning about the history of Oxford and Oxford's mice. Oxford is a nice place to live although it can be quite upsetting to live through so much history. I hope I did not bore you too much.

All in all, Oxford is a pretty cool place to live. In the end, I wouldn't want to live anywhere else.

The End
William McMouse

1936 MG